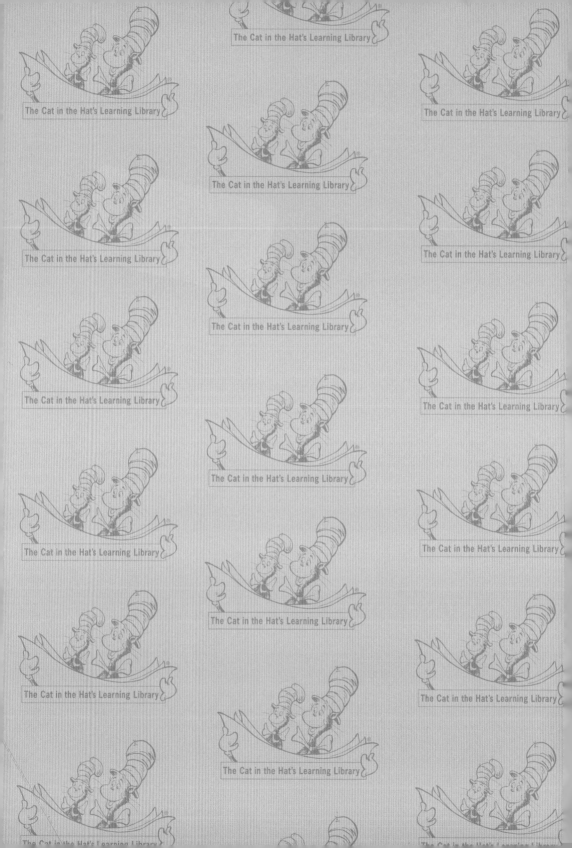

The editors would like to thank
BARBARA KIEFER, Ph.D.,
Charlotte S. Huck Professor of Children's Literature,
The Ohio State University, and
JIM BREHENY,
Director, Bronx Zoo,
for their assistance in the preparation of this book.

First published in the UK by HarperCollins Children's Books in 2011
3 5 7 9 10 8 6 4 2
ISBN: 978-0-00-743305-6

Printed and bound in Hong Kong

A GREAT DAY FOR PUP

by Bonnie Worth

illustrated by Aristides Ruiz

The Cat in the Hat's Learning Library®

HarperCollins *Children's Books*

It's a great day for pup
and for joey and calf.
A great day to learn.
A great day to laugh.

I have fixed up a jeep
that could not be sweeter.
It's my Super-de-Duper
Wild Animal Greeter!

6

Climb in, Dick and Sally.
It is time now to go
to wherever on earth
the wild babies grow.

The motor is racing!
And it is no wonder.
We have a long trip to . . .

. . . Australia—down under!

Ma Kangaroo's pouch
is safe as a purse.
It's where her joey
will grow and will nurse

Joey will stay there
until it is grown
to the size when it can
go out on its own.

A new joey is tiny.
To show what I mean,
Thing One will hold up
this red kidney bean.

These ostrich parents
seem to know best
the way to watch over
the eggs in their nest.

Just like some humans,
I guess you might say:
Dad works the night shift,
while Mum works the day.

When the chicks hatch,
they get up and go
off to learn lessons.
They march in a row.

Intro to Bug Hunting.

Plants to Eat 101.

The chicks learn to kick

and they learn how to run.

When a predator comes,

Dad knows just what to do.

He runs in zigzags, flaps

his wings, and says BOOO-OOO!

What is a predator?
I hear you ask me.
A predator's a
natural enemy!

And here is a mum who
might give you a shock
with her rows of sharp teeth.
Yes, this mum is a croc!

For seventy days,
she watches her nest.
She even stops eating!
Won't take time to rest!

The baby crocs hatch
while under the ground.
Their mum digs them up
when they let out this sound.
UH! UH!

Then she opens up **wide**,
lets them all crawl inside,
and at the bank of the river
they take their first ride.

And now for more babies
to really amaze ya,
we'll journey up north . . .

. . . to the forests of Asia!

Here, Panda Mum gives
her cub sweet loving care.
She has to. It's blind—
and has almost no hair!

She feeds her cub milk
and she cuddles it tight.
For months, she won't let
that cub out of her sight.

Thing One has a chart
on which he will show
just how fast this cute
panda baby will grow.

At one month, the baby
can't do much at all.
At four months, it is
just beginning to crawl.

At seven months, it
can climb and can chew
on the fast-growing plant
that we know as bamboo.

For three years, this tigress
watches over her brood.
She keeps them all warm and
she hunts down their food.

A swat at Mum's tail
might look just like play,
but cub's learning the skills
that she needs to hunt prey.

And just what is prey?
I hate to sound crude,
but prey is an animal
hunted for food.

This elephant mum
gives birth with a THUNK.
Then she helps her calf stand
on all fours with her trunk.

She teaches it how to
stay cool and survive—
where the mud wallows are,
where the tasty plants thrive.

When the elephant mum
finds her job a bit smothering,
a young gal helps out.
This is called allomothering.

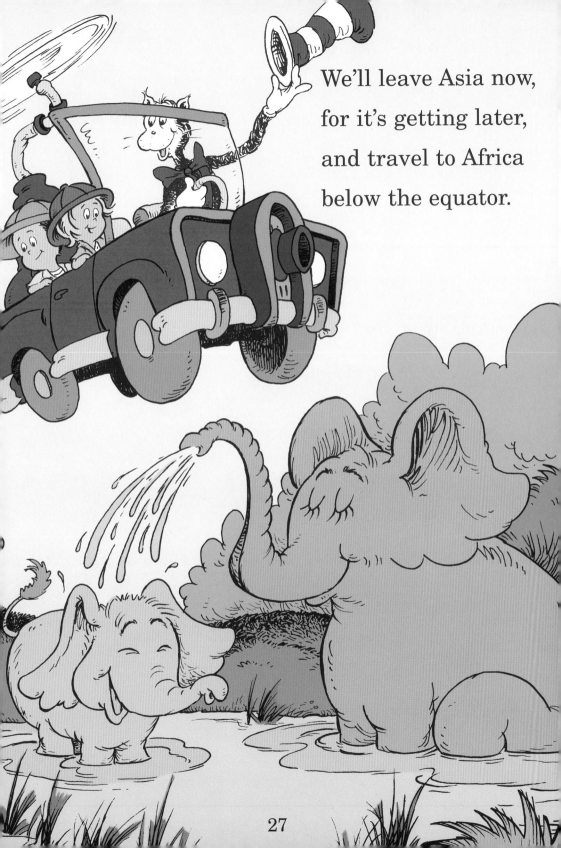

We'll leave Asia now,
for it's getting later,
and travel to Africa
below the equator.

How many babies
do we have on hand
in this troop of gorillas,
who live in a band?
Three baby gorillas,
who get lots of hugs.
Their mums groom their fur
and check them for bugs.

The troop likes to move,
but when baby needs rest,
the mother gorilla
will build it a nest.

And look over there!
Why, it's Mother Giraffe.
And she's just given birth
to a cute giraffe calf.

Already he's standing!
When he wants to eat,
he will open up wide
and let out a bleat.

You'll never believe this,
but I have been told:
giraffes go to kindergarten
at just two weeks old!

31

And what have we here?
A zebra colt—yipes!
But where did it get
all those brown stripes?

The stripes turn black later.
Now it must run fast.
If a colt cannot run,
a colt will not last.

Now we are going
to where it is cold
to visit some chicks who
are just two weeks old.

This baby king penguin
looks ever so sweet,
cuddled all cosy
between Daddy's feet.

The chicks want to eat.

They want to eat now.

(In an hour, they eat

over two pounds of chow!)

Here's a polar bear fact that
I think you should know:
cubs are born in a den
deep under the snow!

At three months of age,
they all squeeze outside,
where the cubs like to romp
and tumble and slide.

It's a great day for pup
and her sea lion mother.
But Mum and her pup
are so far from each other!

They bark back and forth.
They are really quite loud.
And that way the pup
won't get lost in the crowd.

It's time to go now.

It's time to say bye.

Please don't be sad, Sally.

Oh, Dick, please don't cry.

I will fix up your garden.

I will do it for you.

Your mother will not

mind at all if I do.

So, please take my hand.

It is time now to enter

your very own

wild baby . . .

... NURSERY CENTRE!

GLOSSARY

Allomother: A female animal who helps a mother care for her young.

Bleat: An animal noise that sounds like a sad cry.

Brood: A group of young born or hatched at the same time.

Crude: Raw or blunt and lacking in smoothness.

Den: The lair or shelter of a wild animal.

Equator: A circle around the Earth that is an equal distance between the North and South Poles.

Groom: To clean by removing dirt or parasites from the fur, skin, feathers, etc.

Joey: A young animal, usually a kangaroo.

Kindergarten: A group of young giraffes, usually cared for briefly by a single female giraffe.

Predator: An animal that hunts and catches other animals for food.

Prey: An animal hunted or caught for food.

Thrive: To grow quickly and well; flourish.

Troop: A group of animals, usually primates.

Wallow: A dusty or muddy place where wild animals go to roll around in order to cool down or make themselves comfortable.

INDEX

Africa, 27
allomothering, 26
Asia, 18, 27
Australia, 8

bamboo, 21

calves, 6, 24–25, 30, 31
chicks, 11, 12, 34–35
colts, 32–33
crocodiles, 14–17
cubs, 18, 19, 20–21, 22, 23, 36, 37

eggs, 10
elephants, 24–26
equator, 27

giraffes, 30–31
gorillas, 28–29

joeys, 6, 8–9

kangaroos, 8–9
king penguins, 34–35

ostriches, 10–13

pandas, 18–21
penguins, *see* king penguins
polar bears, 36–37
predators, 13
prey, 23
pups, 6, 38

sea lions, 38

tigers, 22–23

zebras, 32–33